MAKERS
As Innovators

W9-DGU-255

Scratch

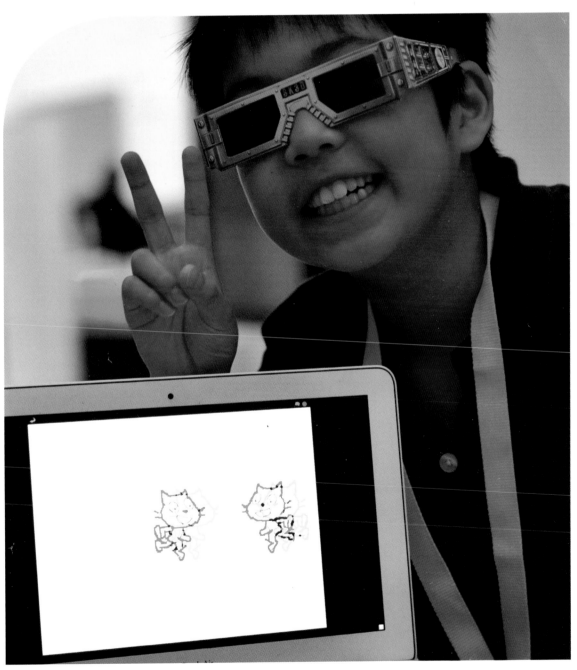

CHERRY LAKE PUBLISHING • ANN ARBOR, MICHIGAN

by Pete Benson

A Note to Adults: Please review the instructions for the activities in this book before allowing children to do them. Be sure to help them with any activities you do not think they can safely complete on their own.

A Note to Kids: Be sure to ask an adult for help with these activities when you need it. Always put your safety first!

Published in the United States of America by Cherry Lake Publishing
Ann Arbor, Michigan
www.cherrylakepublishing.com

Series Editor: Kristin Fontichiaro

Library of Congress Cataloging-in-Publication Data
Benson, Pete, 1960–
  Scratch / by Pete Benson.
  pages cm. — (Makers as innovators) (21st century skills innovation library)
Includes bibliographical references and index.
ISBN 978-1-63362-377-4 (lib. bdg.) — ISBN 978-1-63362-433-7 (pdf) —
ISBN 978-1-63362-405-4 (pbk.) — ISBN 978-1-63362-461-0 (ebook)
1. Scratch (Computer program language)—Juvenile literature. 2. Computer games—Programming—Juvenile literature. I. Title.
QA76.73.S345B46 2016
794.8'1526—dc23   2015009477

Cherry Lake Publishing would like to acknowledge the work of the Partnership for 21st Century Skills. Please visit *www.p21.org* for more information.

Printed in the United States of America
Corporate Graphics
July 2015

Contents

Chapter 1

What Is Scratch?

Every day, we are surrounded by devices such as smartphones, tablets, and laptops. All of these things allow you to interact with computer programs and other content made by talented creators. But what if you want to be the creator? How do you make the games, animations, and other fun things you enjoy on electronic devices?

Mitch Resnick is a computer scientist at the MIT Media Lab in Cambridge, Massachusetts, where he leads the Lifelong Kindergarten Group. He noticed that "young people today have lots of experience ... interacting with new technologies, but a lot less so of creating [or] expressing themselves with new technologies. It's almost as if they can read but not write."

Resnick decided to do something about this. He wanted all people, including kids, to have fun telling stories, creating games, bringing ideas to life, and sharing their work with the rest of the world. To help meet this goal, he and his team developed Scratch.

Scratch is a **programming language.** This means it is a language for giving instructions to a computer. Like human languages, programming languages have vocabulary and grammar rules. This can make them very challenging to learn. Scratch, however, is designed to be easy to learn. It is friendly to new users, even if they don't have any programming experience.

Scratch's mascot is a cat named Scratchy (see right). Scratchy is a sprite. Sprites are objects that can move, change appearance, and allow interaction. They are the most important part of a Scratch project. Any time you create a new project, Scratchy appears as your first sprite.

Coding with Blocks and Scripts

Typical programming languages require you to type **code** that follows strict rules. If you don't follow these rules, the computer can't understand what you want, and your program will not run. Scratch is much simpler. It lets you create projects by simply snapping blocks together. To the right are some examples of blocks.

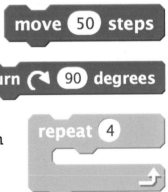

Blocks tell the computer what to do with the sprites you put in your project. The *move 50 steps* block moves a sprite 50 steps. The *turn right 90 degrees* block makes a sprite turn 90 degrees on the screen. The *repeat 4* block snaps around other blocks. Anything inside it will happen over and over until it has happened four times.

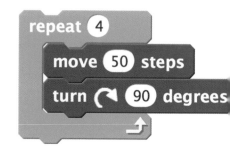

The numbers in the blocks can be changed to adjust the blocks' behavior. You can also snap blocks together into a larger unit called a script. For example, if you made a script using the blocks shown here, Scratchy the sprite will move 50 steps and turn 90 degrees, then repeat these movements four times. When he is done moving, Scratchy will have traced a box shape.

Unlike regular computer code, your Scratch scripts will never confuse the computer. It is not possible to create a block or combine blocks in a way that can be misunderstood.

Categories of Tools

Most programming languages start life with a small set of commands. At first, the language isn't very powerful. Then programmers start writing code to make it more useful. This new code is gathered into collections called libraries. These can be very helpful. However, you need to know what is available in each library and how to find what you need. Scratch comes with a specific set of blocks in its library. They are grouped and color coded according to what they do. This makes it easy to find what you need.

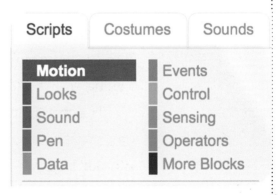

There are 10 categories of blocks. The *move* and *turn* blocks you've already seen are from the *Motion* category. The *Looks* category lets you change the appearance of your sprites. They can tell a sprite to grow, shrink, change colors, and more. *Sound* helps you give your sprites a voice. You can make your sprite draw on the screen using *pen* blocks. *Data* introduces **variables**, which are used to keep track of information about your sprites and your project. *Events* are used to start actions. *Control* refers to control structures. Control structures are commands that tell the computer to repeat a set of instructions or to follow instructions only if a certain condition is met. You learned about your first control structure when we used the *repeat* block. *Sensing* allows you to detect when things happen in your project so your sprites can react. You'll learn more about all of these blocks later in this book.

Hosting Your Application

One thing that sets Scratch apart from other programming languages is that all of the projects you write are automatically saved to the **cloud**. This allows you to log in and access your projects from any computer as long as you have an Internet connection. The cloud also makes it easy to share your projects with others. Users all around the world can view, copy, and even remix the projects you share.

People who create Scratch projects are called Scratchers, and they have shared more than eight million projects so far on the Web. When you are ready to share a project with the world, all you need to do is click the Share button.

A Cross-Platform Language

Most programming languages are available on multiple platforms. In other words, a language can be used to write programs for different **operating systems**, such as Microsoft Windows or Apple OS X. However, a program written for one platform may require a lot of work to get running on other platforms. Luckily, when you create a Scratch project on your computer, it will automatically run on any operating system. In the future, you will even be able to access your projects on smartphones, tablets, and other mobile devices. A version of Scratch for younger kids, called Scratch Jr., is already available for iPads.

Chapter 2

Getting Started

All of your projects will be created directly on the Scratch Web site (*https://scratch.mit.edu*). The first thing you need to do when you visit the site is create an account. To do this, click the Join Scratch button on the site's home page.

You will need to create a username and password. For your online safety, do not use your real name as your username. After this, you must provide a real e-mail address. Ask your teacher if there is an address he or she would like you to use. If you forget your password, Scratch will use this e-mail address to send you a new one.

Once you have created a new account and logged in, click the Create link at the top of the page.

This takes you to the Scratch development environment.

Now you can get started with your very first Scratch project!

Starting a Project

We are going to make a video game. In this game, you will control a spaceship and fire a laser to destroy incoming space rocks. Give your game a descriptive name in the upper left of the screen.

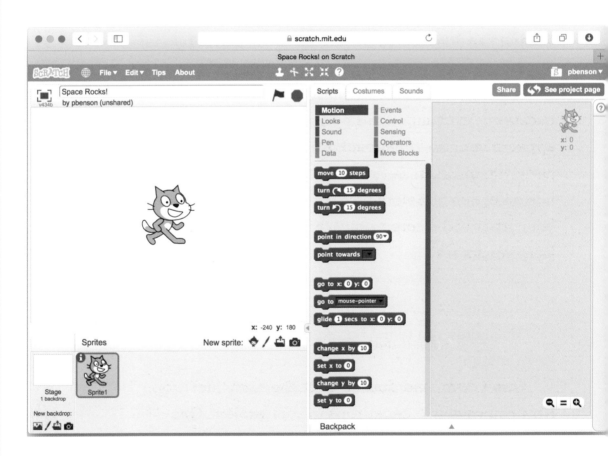

When writing computer programs, it is important to start simply and make gradual improvements. You will notice that as we create our game, we are constantly revising or adding to our program. These small changes will add up to create something big.

Setting the Stage

Scratch programs run in a space called a stage. You can set different *backdrops* to change the stage's appearance. The initial backdrop is just a white screen. Let's make it look like outer space. Select *New Backdrop* from the bottom left corner of the screen, and then choose a backdrop from the library:

Scroll down and double-click the *stars* backdrop. Now you have two backdrops in your project. One is named *backdrop 1*, and the other is named *stars*. Their **icons** are displayed in the center near the top of the screen. We don't need *backdrop1*, so select its icon from the center of the screen and click the small *x* to delete it.

While we're at it, let's create another backdrop to use as a Game Over screen. Choose a new backdrop of your choice from the library. If you see a *Convert to vector* button near the bottom right of the screen, click it. (If the button says *Convert to bitmap*, leave it alone.)

Convert to vector

Now select the *text* tool. This is a button along the right side of the screen that is marked with a *T*.

Click anywhere on the backdrop and add the words "Game Over" to your screen. You can select different **fonts**, resize the text, or change its color if you wish. In the upper left of the backdrop editor, change the name of the backdrop to *Game Over*.

Test, Test, Test!

Test your code often, even if you only make a small change. This will help you catch your mistakes as soon as you make them, instead of much later when it might be more difficult to go back and make corrections. Frequent testing will help you get your programs up and running more quickly.

Chapter 3

Putting It All Together

N ow that our backdrops are ready, it's time to add sprites to the project. The first sprite we will create is a spaceship. Each sprite has a name and can have any number of costumes. Costumes are different appearances the sprite can have. Each sprite needs at least one costume so it can appear on the screen. You can create your own sprite costumes, but let's start by grabbing one of the sprites included in Scratch's library. Click the *Choose Sprite from Library* button to open the sprite library.

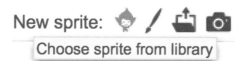

Select the *Spaceship* sprite costume.

Click OK. You should now have two sprites in the panel at the bottom left of the screen. You don't

need Scratchy anymore. Right-click or control-click on his icon, and choose Delete.

Now let's make your spaceship move. Click on the spaceship's icon at the bottom of the screen, then select the *Motion* category in the center near the top of the screen.

Drag a *move 10 steps* block into the script area on the right side of the screen. Click on the block. Your spaceship will move 10 steps.

Notice that the spaceship moves to the right even though it points upward. We can fix this by rotating the costume to match the spaceship's direction. Click on the *Costumes* tab near the top of the screen.

You will see your spaceship's image in the costume editor. Click on the image to select it. Handles for stretching and rotating the image will appear.

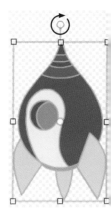

The rotation handle is at the top of the spaceship. Drag it clockwise until the spaceship costume is pointing to the right.

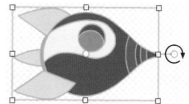

Now we need to make it so players can control the spaceship while playing the game. For this, we need to create a script. A script is a set of instructions for the sprite. When the user presses the up arrow on the keyboard, we want the sprite to move forward. With your spaceship sprite selected, click on the *Scripts* tab.

We are going to use the *move 10 steps* block you added earlier. We only want the spaceship to move if the user is holding down the up arrow. Choose the *Sensing* category.

Scripts

Drag out the *key space pressed?* block. Click the arrow next to the word "space," and a menu of options will drop down. Choose "up arrow" from the drop-down menu.

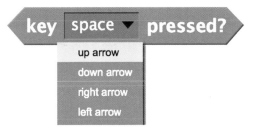

From the *Control* category, drag out an *if-then* block and a *forever* block.

From the *Events* category, grab a *when green flag clicked* block.

From the *Events* category, grab a *when green flag clicked* block.

Now click and drag the pieces to snap them together into this script:

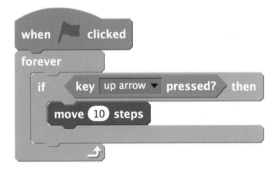

Starting and Stopping Your Program

When you first open a Scratch program, it isn't running. To get it started, click the green flag. To stop the program, click the stop sign. Sometimes you will make changes that require you to restart the program. To do this, just click the green flag again.

Test your program by clicking on the green flag above your game screen. When you press the up arrow key, your spaceship should move across the screen. When you release the up arrow key, your spaceship immediately stops.

At this point, you might ask yourself if this is how you want your spaceship to work. Shouldn't the spaceship gradually speed up as you hold down the key? Let's revise our program by allowing the move size to increase while we are holding down the up arrow key. To do this, we will use a variable. First, click on your spaceship sprite. Then, from the *Data* category, click *Make a Variable*. Name it *moveSize* and choose *For this sprite only*.

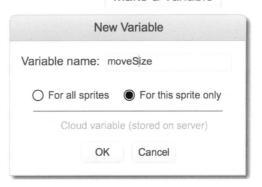

Variables

A variable allows you to keep track of numbers associated with your program. For example, you might use a score variable to track the game score or a *counter* to keep track of the number of lives remaining. If more than one sprite will need to know about the variable, then when you create a variable, select *For all sprites*. Otherwise, select *For this sprite only*.

From the *Data* category, drag a *set moveSize to 0* block, a *moveSize* block, and a *change moveSize by 1* block into the script area.

Now rearrange and edit your spaceship script to look like this:

Notice that we modified *change moveSize by 1* to *change moveSize by 0.1.* This gives the spaceship a gentle acceleration. When the green flag is clicked, the program first makes sure that the spaceship starts out not moving. Then the spaceship enters a *forever* loop, repeatedly checking to see if the up arrow is pressed. If it is, it increases the *moveSize* slightly. Test your script by clicking the green flag.

Our spaceship should move more smoothly now. The only problem is that we can only move it in one direction. Let's modify the script so the spaceship will slow down when we press the down arrow or turn when we press the left and right arrows. Modify your script again to look like the code to the right.

```
when [flag] clicked
set moveSize ▼ to 0
forever
    move moveSize steps
    if  key up arrow ▼ pressed?  then
        change moveSize ▼ by 0.1
    if  key down arrow ▼ pressed?  then
        change moveSize ▼ by -0.05
    if  key left arrow ▼ pressed?  then
        turn ↺ 8 degrees
    if  key right arrow ▼ pressed?  then
        turn ↻ 8 degrees
```

Test it out by clicking the green flag. Now the spaceship repeatedly checks whether the up, down, left, or right arrows are pressed. It speeds up when you press the up arrow and slows down when you press the down arrow. It also turns left when you press the left arrow and right when you press the right arrow. You've got a fully controllable ship!

Missiles

Now we need to create missiles for our ship to fire. We could grab a sprite from the library like we did to make the ship, but this time, let's make a brand-new one. Click the *Paint new sprite* button to open the sprite editor.

You now have a blank canvas for drawing your sprite. The missile is going to be very simple: a filled-in circle. Start by clicking the *Convert to vector* button at the lower right of the sprite editor window.

Now choose a color for the missile. Select the *color a shape* tool and pick a color.

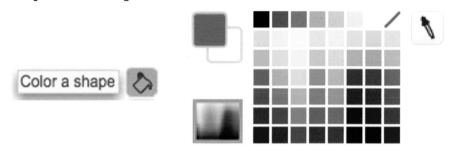

Now select the *ellipse* tool and draw a circle in the middle of the costume editor screen.

Now select the *color a shape* tool again and click inside your circle to fill it in.

Now select the missile sprite from the sprites panel at the bottom left of the screen.

"Sprite2" isn't a very descriptive name. Click the info button at the upper left of your sprite icon. Now change the name of your sprite to Missile. Click the blue arrow to close out the box when you're done renaming.

Now we want to make the missile fire when the player presses the space bar. That doesn't sound too hard. However, we want to be able to shoot many missiles, and we only have one sprite. We need to create clones of our missile sprite. The sprite you have created can be thought of as the master sprite. It will never be displayed. Whenever the master missile detects that the space bar is pressed, it will create a clone.

Click on your missile sprite, then select the *Scripts* tab. You will need two blocks from the *Looks* category, four *Control* blocks, and a *Sensing* block to detect whether the space bar is pressed. Click on your missile sprite, then click on the *Scripts* tab. Then find and assemble the blocks in this script:

When you click the green flag, the master missile

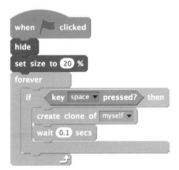

will hide itself and change its size to 20 percent of its original size. It then goes into a loop, repeatedly checking to see if the space bar is pressed. If it is, it clones itself every 0.1 seconds.

The clones will use a separate script from that
of the missile. This script will need to move a clone
to the spaceship, point in the direction of the spaceship, display itself, and then make a sound to indicate
that it fired. Then it starts moving. You will need some
new blocks to create this. The *point in direction of
spaceship* block can be made from one of the *Sensing*
blocks by using the drop-down menus.

You will need a block from the *Sound* category to
play the sound. Finally, we want the clones to go away
if they reach the edge of the screen. You will need
a *Sensing* block that detects whether the missile is
touching the edge.

Here is the assembled script for the clones:

```
when I start as a clone
go to Spaceship ▾
point in direction ( direction ▾ of Spaceship ▾ )
show
play sound pop ▾
forever
    move 6 steps
    if < touching edge ▾ ? > then
        delete this clone
```

Test your script by clicking the green flag.
Pressing the space bar should cause your ship to fire
missiles. Move and turn your ship while firing to verify
that the missiles work as expected.

Chapter 4

Finishing Touches

We have a ship. We have missiles. Now we need something to shoot at! How about rocks? Click the *Choose sprite from library* button and select the *Rocks* sprite.

You will need to create clones of the master *Rocks* sprite, just as we did for the missiles. You want rocks to keep appearing regularly, so we will wait one second between each clone. Your master *Rocks* sprite script should look like this:

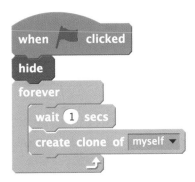

The cloned rocks should not all appear in the same place. Let's have them show up at random locations along the top of the screen. From the *Operators* category, drag out a *pick random 1 to 10* block.

pick random 1 to 10

To use this for a random location, we need to understand a little bit about screen geometry (see sidebar below for more information). Use *the go to x: 0 y: 0* block.

We will set the x-coordinate to a random number between –240 and 240. This means the rock can appear anywhere across the screen. The y-coordinate should stay at 160, near the top of the screen. Combine the two blocks like this:

We could give the rocks a random direction, or we could have them move toward the spaceship. You decide!

point towards Spaceship ▼

The rocks should be different sizes, so let's add a *set size* block with a random percentage between 20 and 40:

set size to (pick random 20 to 40) %

Screen Geometry

Every sprite is located at a point on the screen defined by a numbered grid. This is called a coordinate system. The location coordinates of a sprite consist of two numbers: an x-coordinate and a y-coordinate. The x-coordinate of a sprite can range from –240 on the left side of the screen to 240 on the right side of the screen. The y-coordinate of a sprite can range from –180 on the bottom of the screen to 180 at the top of the screen.

We also might want to have the rocks move at different speeds. Create a *moveSize* variable like you did for the spaceship. Make sure you select *For this sprite only*. This will ensure that every clone gets its own *moveSize* value. Because our master rock is hidden, we also need to make the clones visible with a *show* block from the *Looks* category.

We need a *forever* block to keep the rock in motion. Inside the *forever* loop, we need to move with *moveSize* steps. If a rock touches the edge of the screen, it should bounce. Grab these blocks:

If the rock is touching a missile, the player should score a point and the rock should be destroyed. To track the score, we will need to create a *score* variable *For all sprites*.

The complete script for the rock clones should look like this:

```
when I start as a clone
go to x: pick random -240 to 240 y: 160
point in direction pick random 1 to 360
set size to pick random 20 to 40 %
set moveSize ▼ to pick random 1 to 3
show
forever
    move moveSize steps
    if on edge, bounce
    if touching Missile ▼ ? then
        change score ▼ by 1
        delete this clone
```

Test your script. Rocks should appear randomly at the top of the screen in varying sizes and speeds. You should be able to score points by shooting the rocks with the space bar. We're almost there!

When we created our spaceship, we didn't yet have rocks. Spaceships are supposed to avoid rocks! Let's modify our spaceship script to check for rocks. If a rock hits the ship, the game should end. When the game ends, we would like to see a Game Over screen, and all of the rocks should disappear.

The spaceship needs to sense whether it is has struck a rock. If so, the spaceship is destroyed and the game is over. One way to end the game is to broadcast a message to all sprites so that they can do what they need to do at the end of the game. In the *Events* category, drag out a *broadcast message* block and change its message to "Game Over."

If you want, you can add a sound to your project from the sound library.

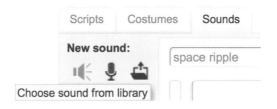

Then from the *Sound* category, drag out a *play sound* block and select your sound.

When the game is over, we should switch to the Game Over backdrop we created in chapter two. We can do this with *a switch backdrop* block from the *Looks* category.

> switch backdrop to gameOver ▼

Putting it together, we add this script to the *forever* loop on our spaceship:

We need the star background to come back when the game starts over. To do this, add a *switch backdrop* block to the beginning of the spaceship script.

> if touching Rocks ▼ ? then
> broadcast Game Over ▼
> play sound space ripple ▼
> switch backdrop to gameOver ▼

> switch backdrop to stars ▼

The rocks should all disappear when the game ends, and cloning new rocks should stop, so add this script to the *Rocks* sprite:

> when I receive Game Over ▼
> stop other scripts in sprite ▼
> delete this clone

Test it! If you are having difficulties, start by trying to figure out the problem on your own. If you're still stuck after a while, a working example of *Space Rocks* can be found at *https://scratch.mit.edu/projects/48675604*.

What's Next?

You've built a video game! You might want to add more features, such as allowing the player multiple lives, different levels of difficulty, different tools, or additional obstacles. You could even create enemy spaceships that fire back at you. It's up to you and your imagination.

Video games aren't the only projects you can build in Scratch. Browse through the Scratch Web site's Featured Projects section to see what others have done. This is a great source of ideas. You can build new projects from the ground up, or you can remix someone else's project.

Besides being fun, learning Scratch is practical. It is a stepping-stone to becoming a **software** developer. Computer programming is rapidly gaining recognition as an important skill in our modern world. Many Scratchers have gone on to learn other programming languages and write apps for computers and mobile devices. The sky is the limit!

Final Version of Your Scripts

Your spaceship script
should now look like this:

Your rocks scripts
should look like this:

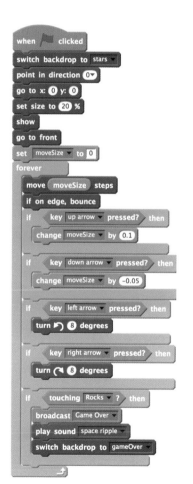

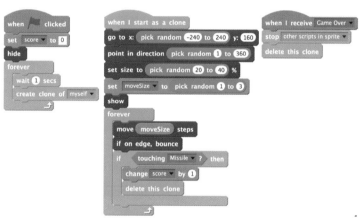

Your missile scripts should look like this:

Glossary

cloud (KLOUD) online storage of digital files so they can be accessed, created, and edited from any computer with an Internet connection

code (KODE) the instructions of a computer program, written in a programming language

fonts (FAHNTS) styles of type

icons (EYE-kahnz) graphic symbols on a computer representing programs, functions, or files

operating systems (AH-puh-ray-ting SIS-tuhmz) software in a computer that supports all the programs that run on it

programming language (PROH-gram-ing LANG-gwij) a language used to give instructions to a computer

software (SAWFT-wair) computer programs that control the workings of the equipment, or hardware, and direct it to do specific tasks

variables (VAIR-ee-uh-buhlz) numbers that can change depending on other circumstances

Find Out More

BOOKS

Chiu, Yolanda. *Super Scratch Programming Adventure! Learn to Program by Making Cool Games!* San Francisco: No Starch Press, 2014.

Nagle, Jeanne. *Getting to Know Scratch*. New York: Rosen, 2015.

WEB SITES

Scratch: About Scratch
https://scratch.mit.edu/about
Learn more about how Scratch was created and how people are using it around the world.

Scratch: Explore Projects
https://scratch.mit.edu/explore/?date=this_month
Check out some of the projects other people have made using Scratch.

VATORS

Index

About the Author

Pete Benson is a computer science, math, and physics teacher, and a Woodrow Wilson STEM teaching fellow. Before teaching high school, he had careers as a fighter pilot, software developer, and financial engineer working on Wall Street. He earned his PhD in industrial & operations engineering from the University of Michigan. His Web site is *http://mrbenson.org*.